THE DESERT

PETER MACINNIS & JANE BOWRING

illustrated by
KIM GAMBLE

Puffin Books

Just before dawn the desert is cold and dark and quiet.
Nothing stirs, nothing rustles, nothing moves.
The faint glow in the eastern sky casts long shadows across the sand.

It's getting lighter now and
the desert seems empty.
But what are those marks
in the sandy soil, near the rock?
Are they footprints?
And what could have made those strange wriggly lines in the sand?
Or those claw marks?
There must be something hiding,
something sleeping in the desert.

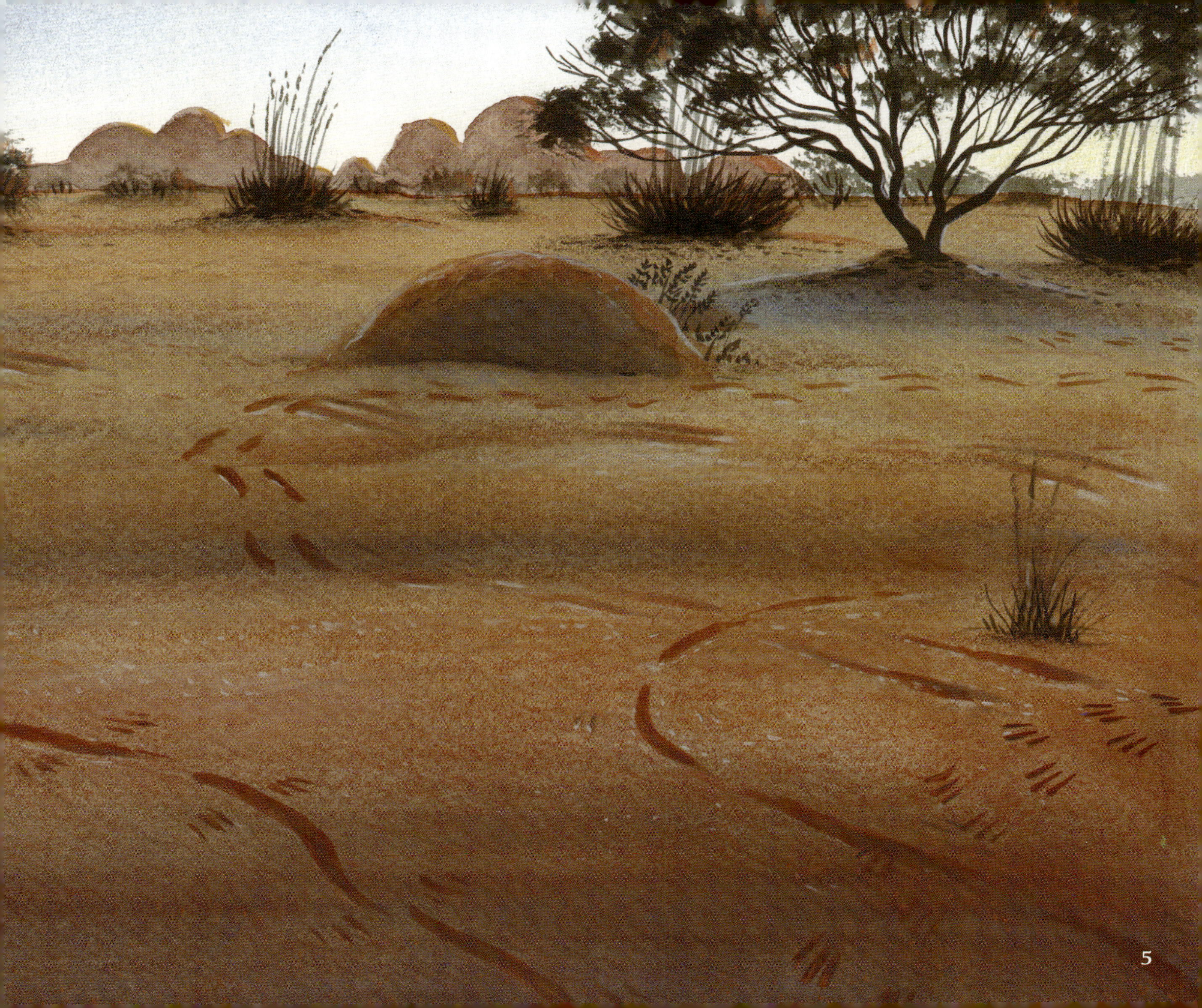

From under a rock slowly slithers a bandy bandy.
It rests in the sun, letting the early morning rays warm its cold blood.
When it soaks up the sun it will be able to move faster.

On the other side of the rocky ridge,
a Children's python makes its way
to its favourite sunny spot.
The lump in its body is yesterday's breakfast.
Pythons swallow animals whole
then digest them in their stomach.

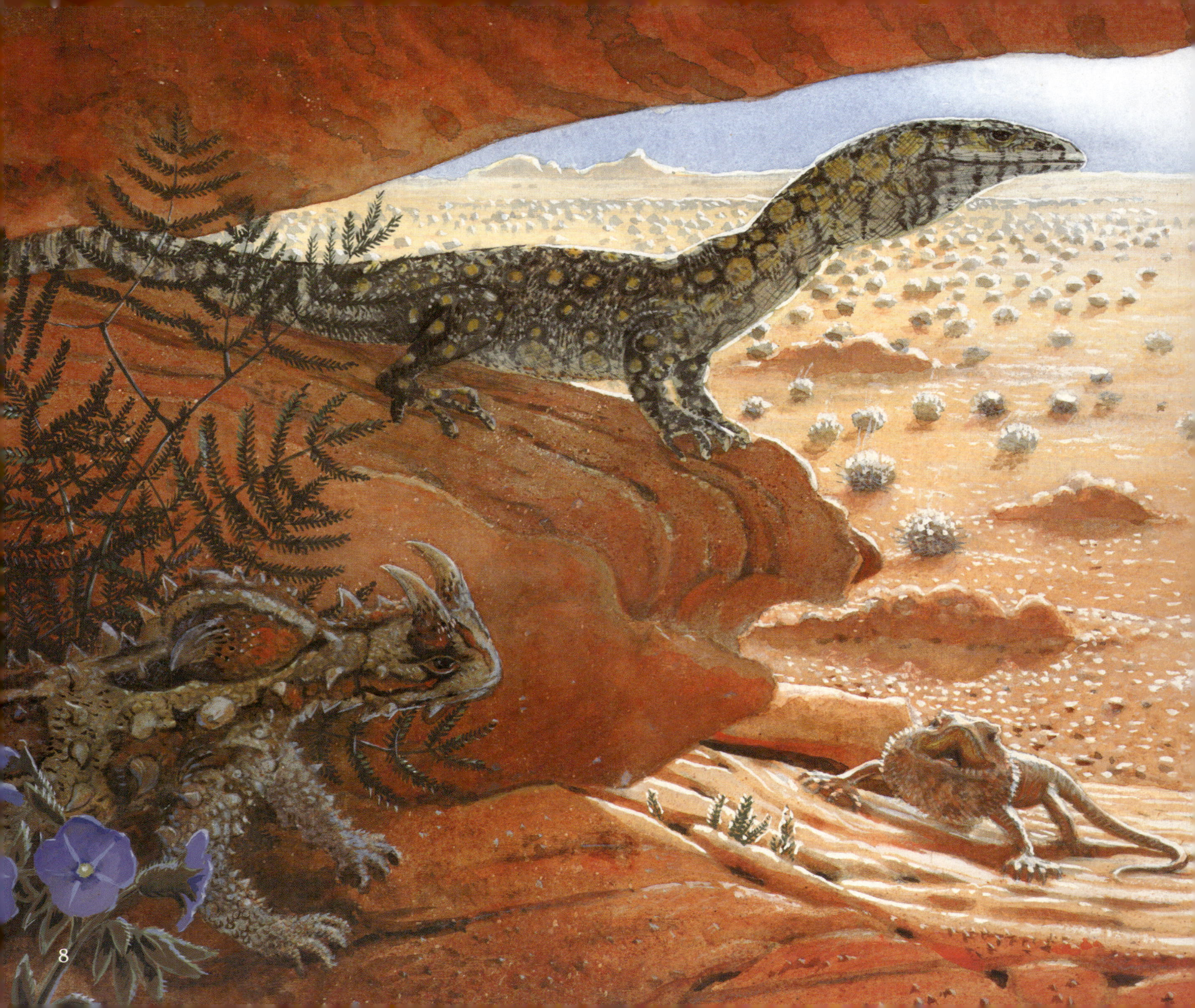

All over the desert goannas, geckos,
skinks, thorny devils and bearded dragons
are beginning to stir.
So are other snakes like the woma
and the poisonous brown.
They come out from under crevices and rocks seeking the sun's warmth.
As soon as the night cold
has gone from their bodies,
the hungry ones will hunt for food.

Now the sun is higher in the sky and
the large soaring birds are beginning to fly.
Hot air rises from the biggest rocks
which have been heated by the sun.
The kites and the hawks whirl round and around
in these currents of air until they are high in the sky.

A fork-tailed kite drifts easily through the air,
searching for its dinner. There's a movement below—
a small animal is scurrying along the ground.

Silently the kite swoops.
As it rises again a wriggling gecko is clutched in its talons.

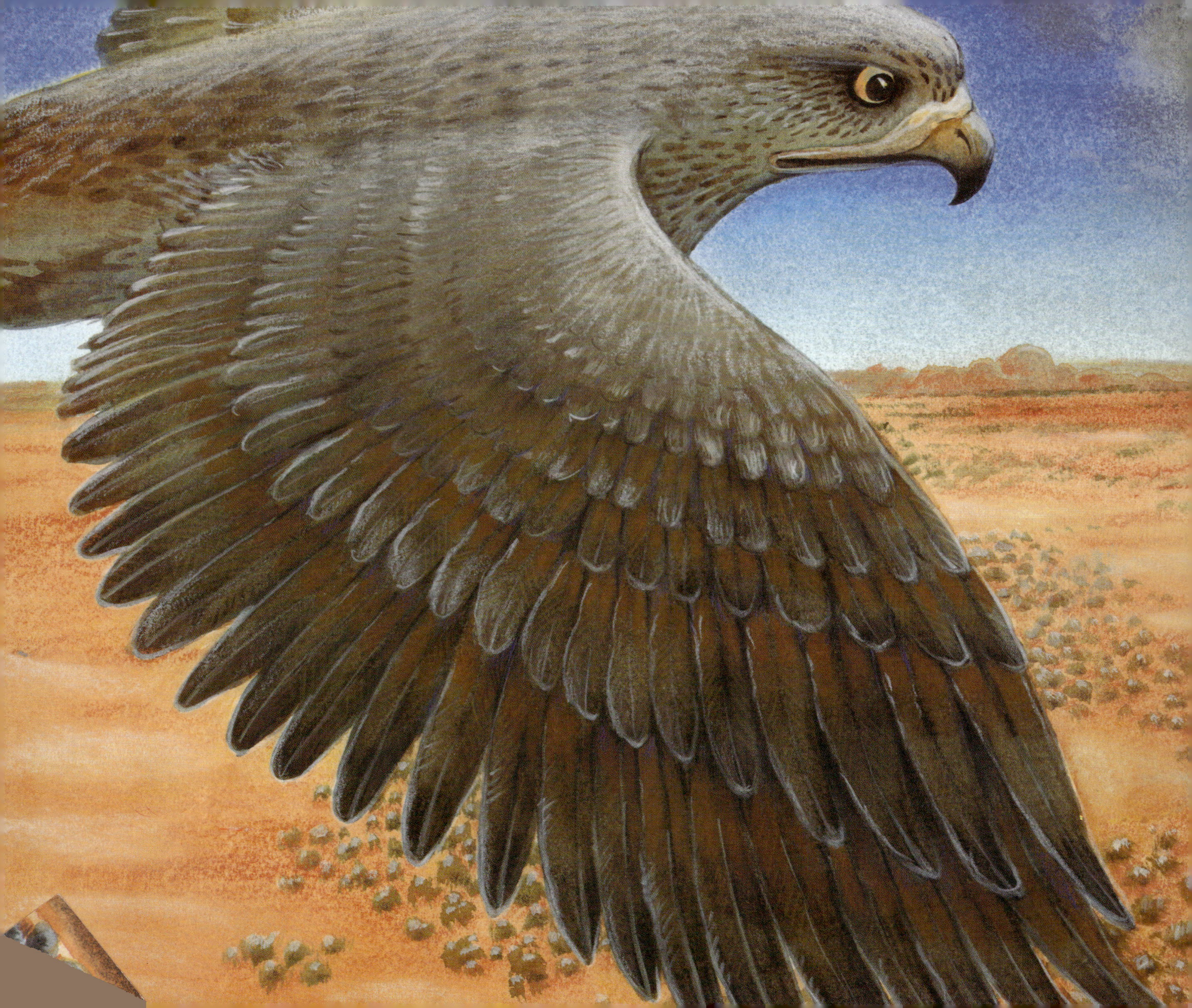

From high above the desert
the kite can see a very long way.
A fork of lightning splits the sky in the east
and soon after the kite sees smoke clouds rising.
A fire is burning in the grasslands.
Fire makes small animals panic and run from cover.
Lazily the kite slides across the sky,
towards the black smoke.
Down it swoops, capturing a fat juicy grasshopper.

14

The fire burns quickly but it dies out
when it reaches the stony desert.
Big drops of rain begin to fall.
The rain will start new life in the warm ashes.
Already fire beetles are moving into the ashes
to lay eggs among the roots of the burnt plants.
Two gibber birds fly down and
eat some of the fire beetles.

Many desert plants have seeds which will
grow only after they have been heated by fire.
The rain will help these seeds to start sprouting,
and soon there will be new plants among the ashes.

Deep underground, burrowing frogs are sleeping.
The rain is heavy enough to soak into the soil,
so the frogs get wet and wake up.
They come out to mate and lay new eggs.

The rain fills the waterholes, and on the clay pans
there will be puddles for a week or two.
Shield shrimps hatch in these puddles.
Before they die, the shrimps will lay eggs.
The eggs will lie in the clay,
waiting for the next rain.

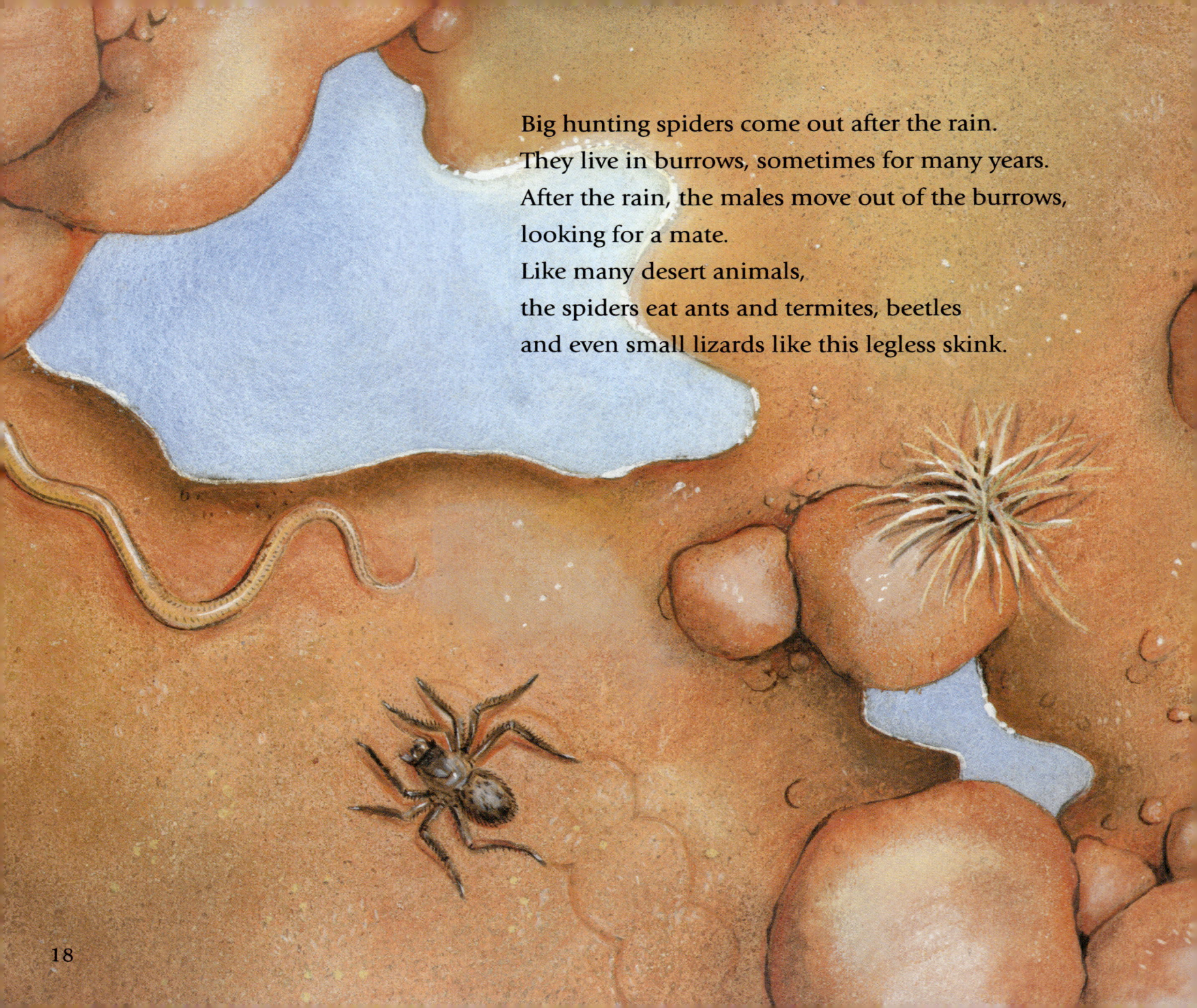

Big hunting spiders come out after the rain.
They live in burrows, sometimes for many years.
After the rain, the males move out of the burrows,
looking for a mate.
Like many desert animals,
the spiders eat ants and termites, beetles
and even small lizards like this legless skink.

This spider had better look out, or the thorny devil will get him!

19

The spider scuttles down into its burrow,
so the thorny devil wanders off looking for ants.
Lots of desert animals like to eat ants.
The thorny devil snaps up a few
but the rest escape safely
back into the nest.
Thousands of ants live in the nest
which goes deep into the ground.

21

Not far from the ant nest is a nest of termites.
Termites are often called white ants.
They eat wood and dead leaves,
things most other animals cannot eat.
There are special 'soldier' termites
which protect the nest from raiders.

Geckos like to eat termites.
They burrow into the nests,
and some lay their eggs inside the termite mound.

The sun is setting.
The larger mammals come out into the cool evening.
A western grey kangaroo hops past the termite nest.
A small plains rat peeps out from a clump of spinifex
where she is feeding her two young with milk.
Soon they will be old enough to eat seeds and insects,
just as she does, but for now they need their mother's milk.

25

When night falls,
and the rocks and sand cool,
the long rabbit ears of the bilby
appear above the sand.
Sniffing the air to make sure
there are no enemies nearby,
it leaves the safety of its deep burrow
to search for food.

Out come tiny hopping mice
to look for seeds and small insects,
and green plants for moisture.
If they see a kowari they bound away.
Kowaris usually eat insects,
but if they see a mouse in the faint starlight,
they stalk it, pouncing on it
and killing it with a bite to the neck.

28

The birds of the night leave no tracks.
With their big dark eyes, the boobooks and barn owls
can see small animals on the ground below.
Silently they swoop,
seizing their dinner with sharp claws.

The dunnart under the log
is looking for insects and small spiders,
but if it isn't careful,
it will become boobook food instead.

Just before dawn the night animals go into hiding—
under rock shelves, down burrows,
behind sheets of bark, beneath rocks
or squeezed into cracks and crevices,
safe from the heat of the sun which will soon rise.

But now the desert is as cold as ice.
The animals of the day still sleep,
waiting for the warmth the new day will bring.

gibber bird, barn owl, boobook, kite, hawk

goanna, thorny devil, legless skink, bilby, kangaroo

bearded dragon, gecko, kowari, dunnart, hopping mouse

Children's python, plains rat, woma

bandy bandy, ant, fire beetle, grasshopper, hunting spider, burrowing frog

shield shrimp